Level
2

The Nature Kid's Guide to
CHEETAHS

RENATA MARIE

LP Media Inc. Publishing
Text copyright © 2023 by LP Media Inc.

For information address LP Media Inc. Publishing, 3178 253rd Ave. NW, Isanti, MN 55040
www.lpmedia.org

Publication Data

Cheetahs
The Nature Kid's Guide to Cheetahs — First edition.

Summary: "Learn all about Cheetahs, the Nature Kid Way"
— Provided by publisher.

ISBN: 978-1-954288-64-5

[1. Cheetahs – Non-Fiction] I. Title.

Title: The Nature Kid's Guide to Cheetahs

CONTENTS

Run Wild 4

Born to Run 6

Built for Speed 8

Meat Eaters 10

Eye Spy 12

Hard to Spot 14

Flying Feet 16

Out of Gas 18

Swipe and a Miss 20

Lazy Days 22

Purring Cubs 24

Hiding Spots 26

Little Hunters 28

Into the World 30

A Losing Race 32

Nowhere Safe 34

Trouble with Humans . . . 36

Race to Live 38

RUN WILD

Whoosh! **Sharp claws rip the sand. Strong legs fly over the land. It's a cheetah!**

Cheetahs live in Africa. They hide in the tall grass. They race over the open land. No animal can outrun them. Cheetahs are the fastest land animals in the world. And they are ready to sink their teeth into their next feast.

Cheetahs can run up to 70 miles (113 kilometers) per hour.

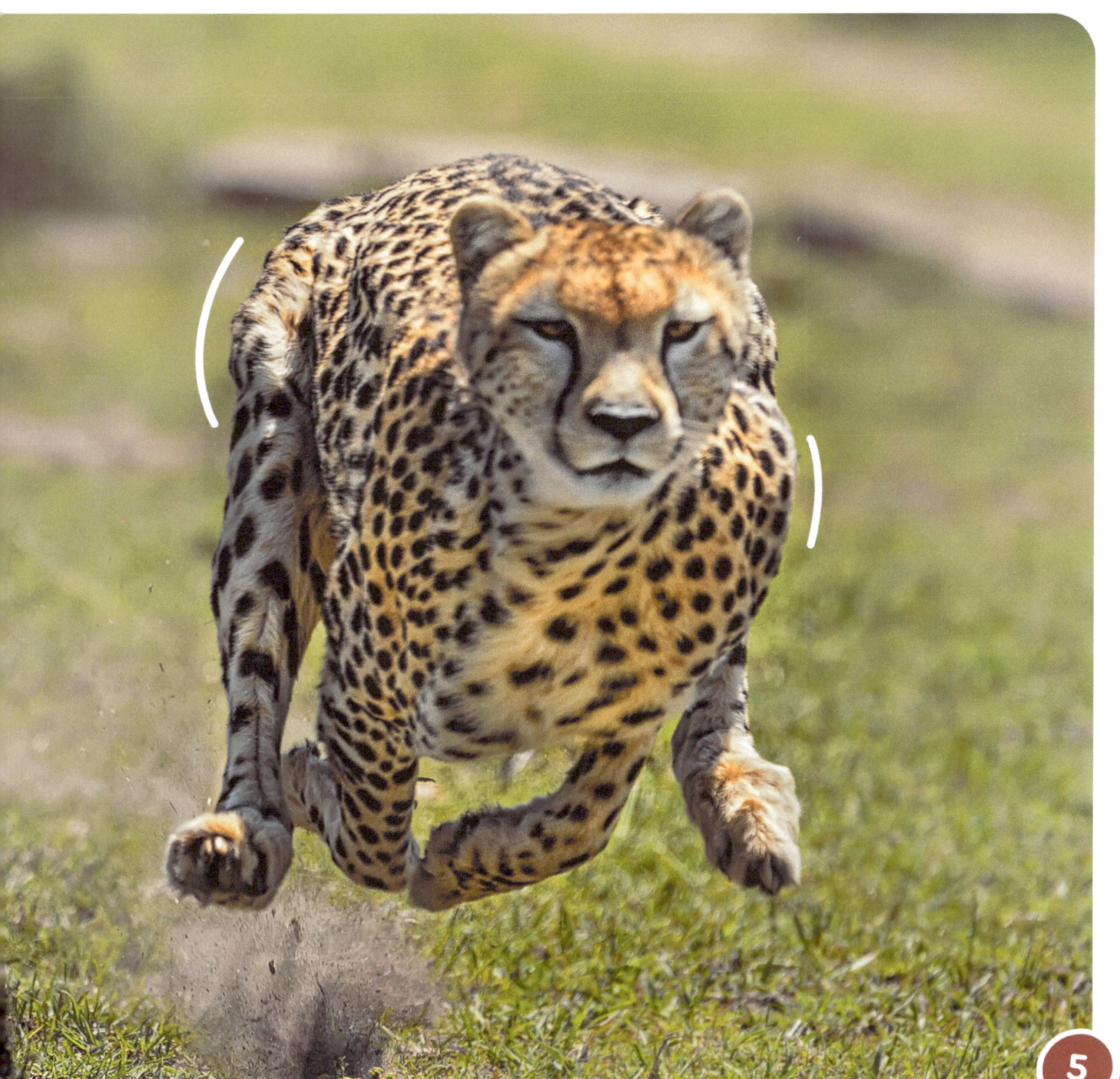

BORN TO RUN

A cheetah races toward a hare. His tail swings. His long body reaches.

Cheetahs are born to run. They are light. They only weigh up to 140 pounds (64 kilograms). They are only three feet (0.9 meters) tall. Males are usually larger than females.

Their tails are long. They help them balance when they run. They help them change direction.

DID YOU KNOW?

Cheetah tails can be 30 inches (76 centimeters) long.

BUILT FOR SPEED

Cheetahs' claws grip the ground. They are like track shoes.

A cheetah charges. Her heart races. Her lungs take in air.

Cheetahs' bodies are built for speed.
Their legs are long. Their chests are deep.
Their noses are wide. Their hearts are big.
Their lungs are big. They breathe a lot of air.
This helps them run fast.

Cheetahs have sharp noses and ears, but they usually use their eyes to hunt. If a cheetah spots an animal, it better start running. Or it might feel the cheetah's sharp teeth.

9

MEAT EATERS

Zebra

Wildebeest

Duiker

Ostrich

Steenbok

Warthog

An antelope runs. Teeth snap at his legs.

Cheetahs are **carnivores**. **They eat meat.** Cheetahs are small. They have to hunt smaller animals. They hunt antelopes. They hunt warthogs, birds, and hares. Sometimes they hunt zebras, wildebeests, and ostriches.

Cheetahs usually cannot take down large animals. But they can catch their young.

EYE
SPY

A cheetah sits on a tall rock. She looks over the land.

Cheetahs use their big eyes to find prey. They sit on a tall rock or hill. Their eyes sit high on their heads. They can easily see over the open land. They can see small prey 3.1 miles (5 km) away. They can see 210 degrees around them.

The black marks under a cheetah's eyes keep the sun out, just like a football player's black marks.

HARD
TO SPOT

The tall grass sways.
Hungry eyes lock on a warthog.

When cheetahs spot prey, they sink into the tall grass. They use **camouflage** to get close to their prey. **Each cheetah has its own pattern of spots.** The spots on their bodies look like shadows in the grass. They help them hide.

Young cheetahs have long fur on their backs. It makes them look like honey badgers. **Predators** do not want to pick a fight with a honey badger.

FLYING
FEET

A cheetah stays close to the ground. She creeps quietly.

Cheetahs get close to their prey before charging. Then they attack.

Cheetahs slice through the air. Their long bodies bend easily. **Their legs can cover over 20 feet (6.1 m) in one stride.** Four strides only take one second.

When close, a cheetah will swipe at its prey's feet. The prey trips and crashes to the ground. The cheetah bites it to keep it down.

Cheetahs run so fast that all of their paws can be in the air at once.

OUT
OF GAS

A cheetah lies next to his catch. But he does not eat.

Africa is hot, and running makes a cheetah even hotter. They can only run for a short time. If they catch their prey, they need to cool down before they eat.

Cheetahs can take 30 minutes to catch their breath. During that time, they have to watch out for other predators. Lions, hyenas, leopards, vultures, and jackals will try to take their catch. And cheetahs are too small to fight back.

Cheetahs hunt during the day to stay away from bigger predators.

SWIPE
AND A MISS
20

Swipe! **A cheetah misses. The antelope gets away.**

Cheetahs may be fast. **But they only catch half of the prey they chase.**

Lone adults only eat every two to five days. But females with baby cheetahs hunt every day. Cheetahs need to eat up to eight pounds (3.6 kg) a day.

Cheetahs only drink water every four days. Sometimes only once every 10 days.

LAZY DAYS

The sun heats the land.
A cheetah rests under a tree.

Cheetahs hunt when the sun is low in the sky. They hunt in the early morning. They hunt in the late afternoon. They want to stay out of the sun.

Cheetahs spend most of their day sleeping. They rest under trees, where it is cool. They watch over their young while they play.

PURRING
CUBS

A baby cheetah purrs. She is warm in her mother's fur.

Baby cheetahs are called cubs. Female cheetahs usually have three to five cubs at a time. They are born helpless. They weigh less than one pound (0.5 kg). They are blind.

Their mother cleans them with licks. She purrs to make them feel safe. She keeps them warm. The cubs drink her milk. She must go hunting. If she does not eat, she cannot make them milk to drink.

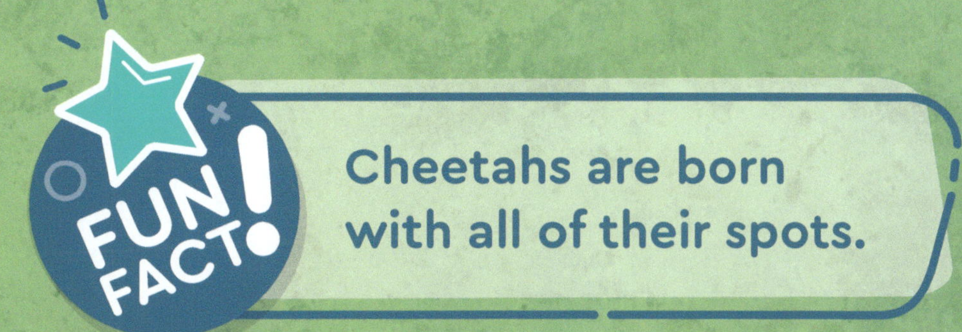

HIDING SPOTS

A cheetah picks up her cub. She hurries to a new hiding spot.

Every few days, mother cheetahs pick new spots to hide their cubs. **Moving makes it harder for predators to smell them.**

Adult cheetahs are hard to catch. But cubs have to watch out for lions, leopards, hyenas, and eagles.

LITTLE HUNTERS

A cub swipes at his brother. His brother nips back.

At six weeks old, cubs start to follow their mothers when they hunt. **Cubs learn to hunt by watching their mothers.**

Cubs also learn by playing. They creep toward each other. They chase. They swipe. They nip. They knock each other down.

Cubs stop drinking milk at four months old. Soon, they will hunt with their mothers.

A cheetah mother brings her cubs live prey. She drops it in front of them and they try to catch it.

29

INTO THE
WORLD

A cheetah pees on a rock. He is telling other cheetahs to stay away.

When cheetahs are 18 months old, they leave their mothers. Females leave to have cubs. And males live together.

Males mark their land. They rub and pee on rocks and trees. They want to keep other male cheetahs off their land. Females cross through the lands to find food.

But there is less land for cheetahs to live on.

Cheetahs growl, chirp, bark, cough, bleat, moan, meow, and hiss.

A LOSING RACE

A cheetah looks for prey. But all he sees are roads and houses.

Cheetahs are vulnerable. There are fewer cheetahs each year. They used to live all over Africa. They lived in parts of Asia.

But people moved in. They hunted the cheetahs' prey. They took over the cheetahs' land.

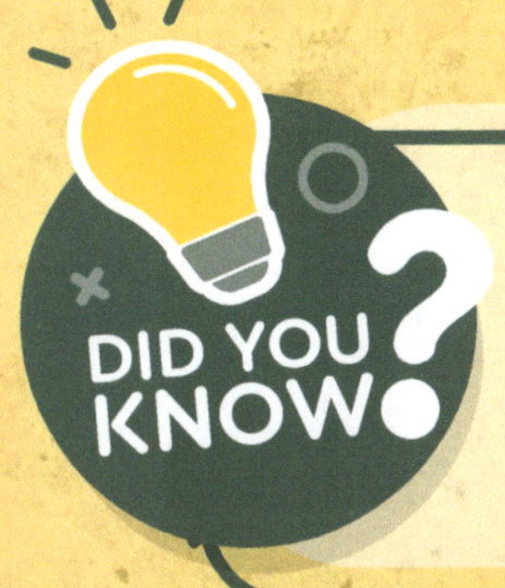

Today, there are less than 8,000 cheetahs in Africa and less than 50 cheetahs in Asia.

NOWHERE SAFE

A cheetah looks for prey. A car drives past. The prey gets away.

As more people moved across Africa, they needed more space. They built towns and roads. They built houses and farms. **But they left less room for the animals.**

Cheetahs need a lot of land. They need safe places to sleep and hunt.

Cheetahs do not do well in protected parks. There are too many larger predators in a smaller space.

TROUBLE WITH HUMANS

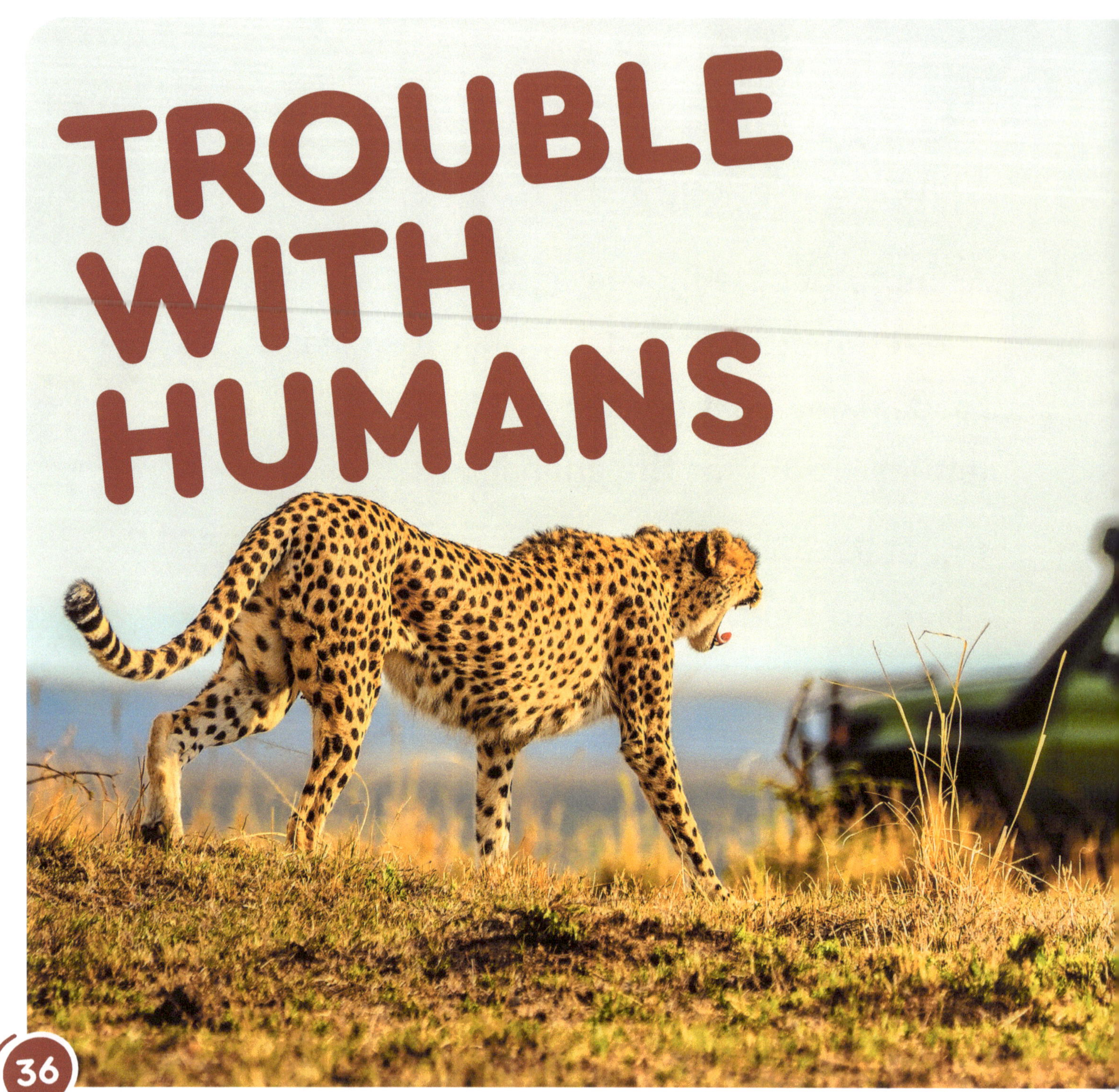

People illegally hunt cheetahs.

They want them for their spotted fur. They want them for their meat. People hunt other animals too. There is less prey for cheetahs to hunt.

Cheetahs are hungry. They hunt farm animals. Farmers try to keep them away. Sometimes cheetahs get hurt.

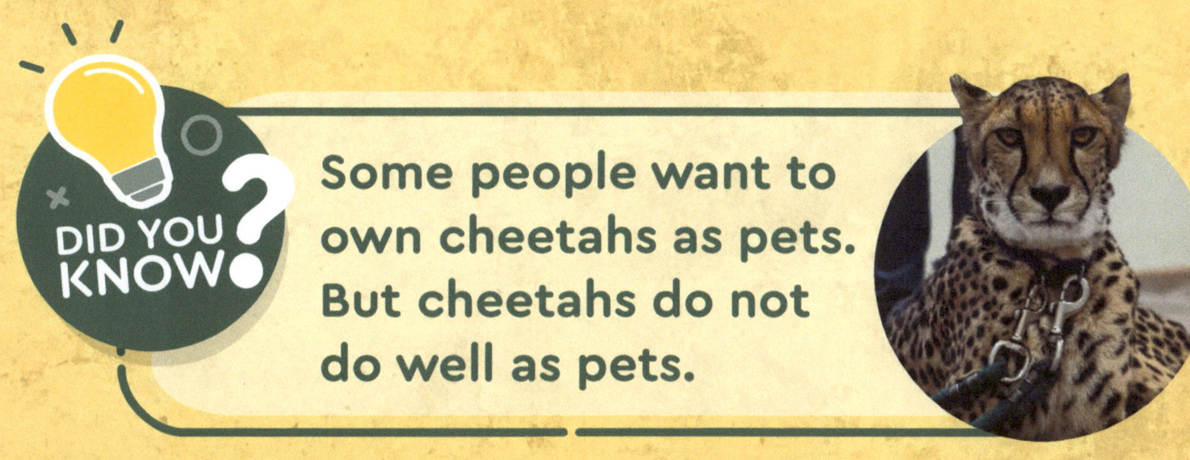

RACE
TO LIVE

A puppy plays with a cheetah. The two are best friends.

People are trying to help cheetahs. People are trying to catch illegal hunters. They help build walls around farm animals. They give farmers dogs. The dogs bark to scare away cheetahs.

Some people want to help cheetahs make more cubs in zoos. But cheetahs do not do well in zoos. They need space to hunt, play, and run wild.

People put dogs with cheetah cubs in zoos. They grow up together. They play together. The dogs help the cheetahs stay calm.

GLOSSARY

camouflage
something that helps
an animal hide
page 15

predators
animals that hunt
other animals
page 15

carnivores
animals that eat meat
page 11

prey
animals that are hunted
by other animals
page 13

stride
when each paw
steps once
page 17

vulnerable
in danger
page 33

MORE AMAZING ANIMAL BOOKS
from Nature Kids Publishing!

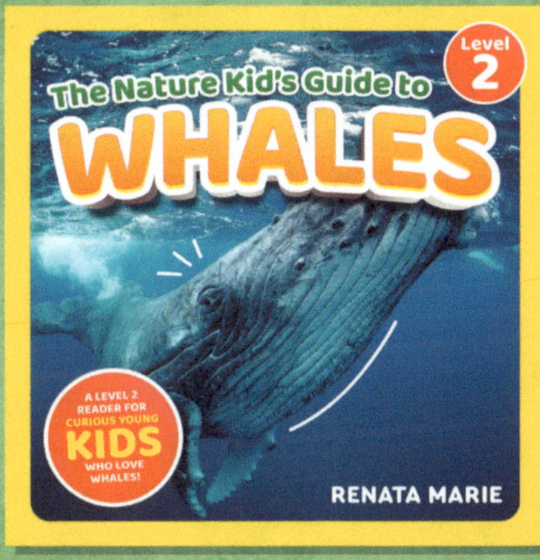

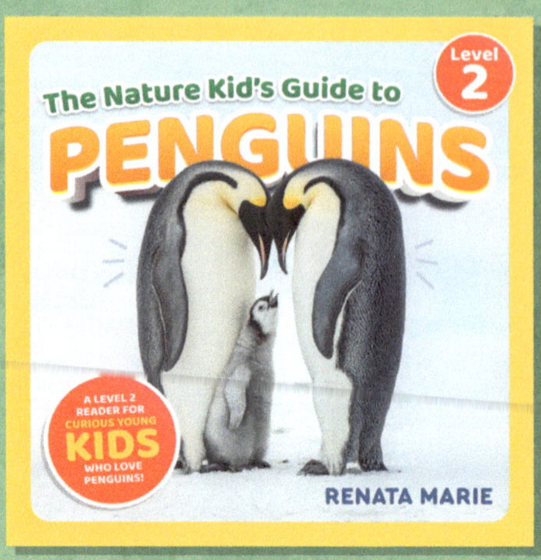

Visit NatureKidsPublishing.com
to Learn More!

www.ingramcontent.com/pod-product-compliance
Lightning Source LLC
Chambersburg PA
CBHW042123030726
47599CB00002B/328